The Dinosaur

Edited by Gillian Doherty
With thanks to Darren Naish for information about dinosaurs

Illustrations copyright © Mandy Field 2004
First published in 2004 by Usborne Publishing Ltd, 83-85 Saffron Hill, London EC1N 8RT, England.
www.usborne.com. Copyright © 2004 Usborne Publishing Ltd. The name Usborne and the devices ♀ ⊕ are Trade Marks
of Usborne Publishing Ltd. All rights reserved. No part of this publication may be reproduced, stored in a retrieval system,
or transmitted in any form or by any means, electronic, mechanical, photocopying, recording or otherwise,
without the prior permission of the publisher. UE. First published in America in 2005. Printed in Dubai.

The Dinosaur

Anna Milbourne

Illustrated by Mandy Field

Designed by Laura Fearn and Laura Parker

Nobody has ever seen a real live dinosaur.

But long, long ago, before the
world had cars or roads...

before there were
houses or cities...

and even before the very
first people were born...

a big, brown dinosaur egg
lay at the edge of a huge forest.

From inside the egg came a tap, tap, tap.

Then there was a

CRACK!

And out climbed a baby stegosaurus.

One by one, more eggs broke open.

His brothers and sisters
were hatching out too.

The baby stegosaurus
was very, **very** hungry.

He ate whatever
he could find.

He ate crunchy cones and ferny leaves,
and chewy fruit from spiky plants.

Each day he grew **bigger** and **bigger**...

until he was almost as big as an elephant.

Soon, the stegosaurus was so big,
he had trouble fitting through the trees.

So he poked his head out of the forest,
to see what the world was like outside.

It seemed safe enough.

But not for long.

Suddenly, he heard a...

ROAR!

It was an **enormous** allosaurus
with **enormous** allosaurus teeth...

and it wanted to eat him up!

The allosaurus growled
and left him alone.

The stegosaurus felt big and strong.
Now he could take care of himself.

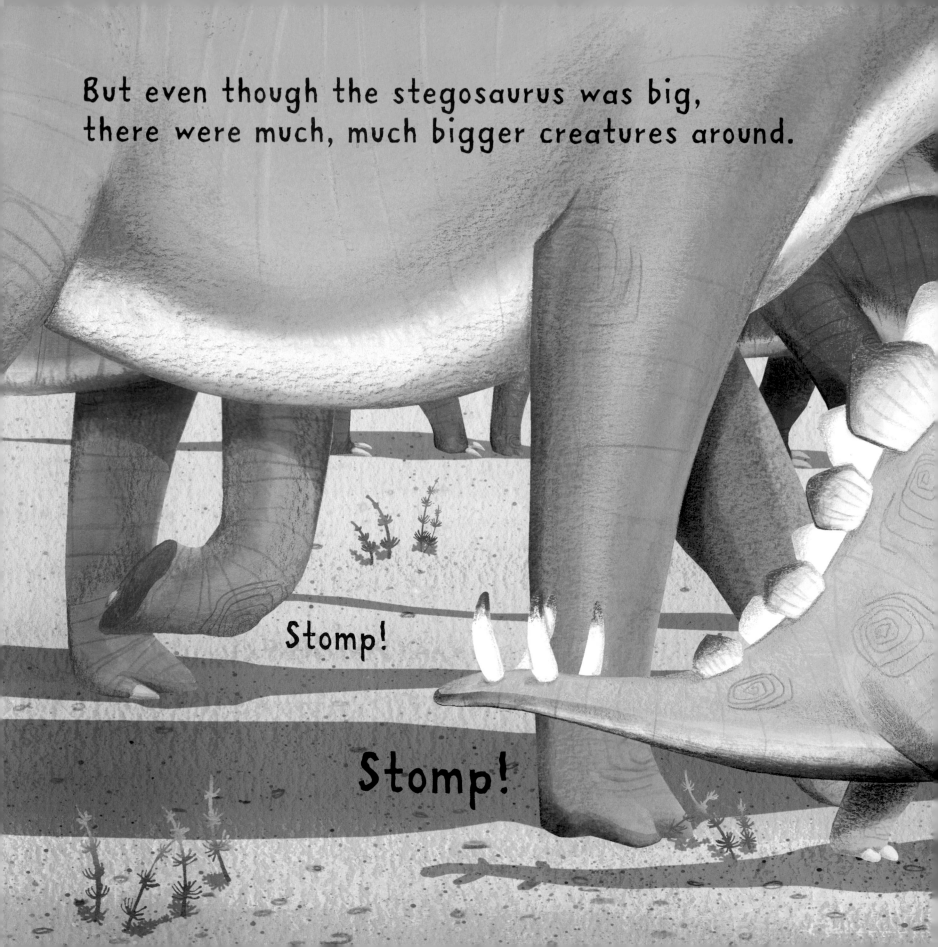

But even though the stegosaurus was big,
there were much, much bigger creatures around.

Stomp!

Stomp!

Stomp!

Stomp!

The ground shook
with giant footsteps.

A whole herd of diplodocuses
was marching across the plains.

Luckily, they only ate leaves...

NOT stegosauruses.

The world was different when dinosaurs lived.

What would it be like if they were still alive?

They would block up roads...

Maybe it's just as well that only their dusty old bones are left.